Barbara

I CAN HELP
ON THE FARM

An 'I Read, You Read' Book

Written and Photographed by: Barbara Linsley
With content approved by:
Audrey Donahoe, Director on the National Dairy Board

Published by:

Whitehall Publishing.
PO Box 548
Yellville, AR 72687

www.whitehallpublishing.com
E-mail info@whitehallpublishing.com

Book Design by:

Ascender Graphix
www.ascendergraphix.com

Printed in China.
Retail Price: $14.95

My heartfelt thanks to the families who opened their farms to me:

Jeffrey and Audrey Donahoe
Seth, Sam and Allison Donahoe

Tim and Colleen Head
Nicole, Cassie and Lacie Head
Natalie, Jenna and Molly Head
Shannon and Adam Schultz

Clayton and Lori Crumb
Caleb Crumb
Noah Bascom

William and Demetria Lunny
Rosetta and Thomas Poveromo
William and Matthew Lunny

Amanda Hibbard
Deysi Ixlaj

My special Thanks to Audrey Donahoe who has provided me with information and checked my work for accuracy and safety.

With the continual loss of farmland and the increasing financial stresses on our family-run diary farms, these kids who care so much about their cows and their family farms deserve our utmost respect and admiration! I hope they carry on the farming tradition.

I can help on the farm!

Farmers grow the crops that feed us. They grow the food we buy in the grocery store. Cows raised on dairy farms give us our milk, butter and ice cream! Farmers take good care of their land so that it will produce food for all of us.

I can help with our tractors.

We have several tractors, big ones and little ones! We have tractors that plow and plant the fields, tractors that pull the manure spreader and tractors we use for haying.

My sisters show me how the tractor works.

I like to ride in the cab with my dad when he goes to get round bales for feeding the cows in the barn.

I can help plow
with our team of horses.

Some farms still use horses. We use horses to pull the plow to show people how farming was done before tractors.

Some people plow with horses because they don't want to use modern machinery.

I can help clean the barn.

The barn floor and the gutters must be cleaned every day.
The gutter has a belt-operated cleaner which carries manure out
to the manure spreader which we pull with a tractor out
to fertilize the fields.

I can help milk the cows.

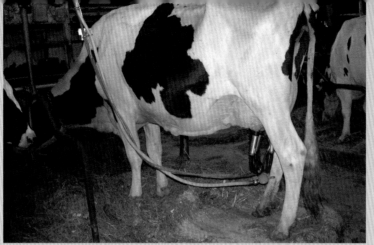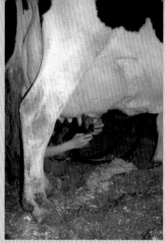

Most cows are no longer milked by hand. Milking machines are used. I can milk a cow, but machines are faster and safer for the person doing the milking. The milking machines also keep the milk cleaner, the milk is never touched. The machine carries the milk directly into the milk room.

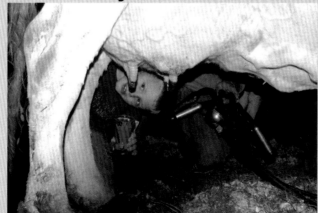

After milking, we dip the cows' udders in iodine. It doesn't hurt. It can prevent painful infections.

I can help in the milk room.

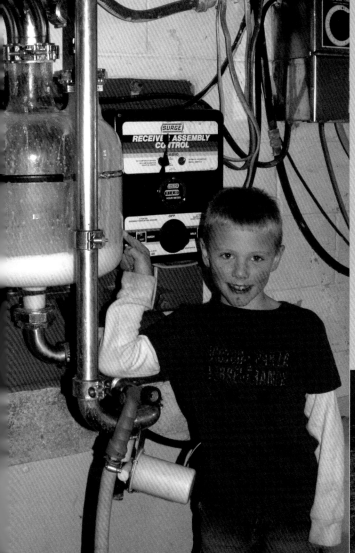

The milk is carried by the milking machine from the cows into this receiving jar in the milk room. It goes through a filter into the main bulk tank which keeps the milk cool until the milk truck gets it.

I can get a drink right from the jar for our cats.

I can get ready for the milk truck.

Our cows give an average of 65 pounds of milk a day! That's 7 ½ gallons of milk from each cow.

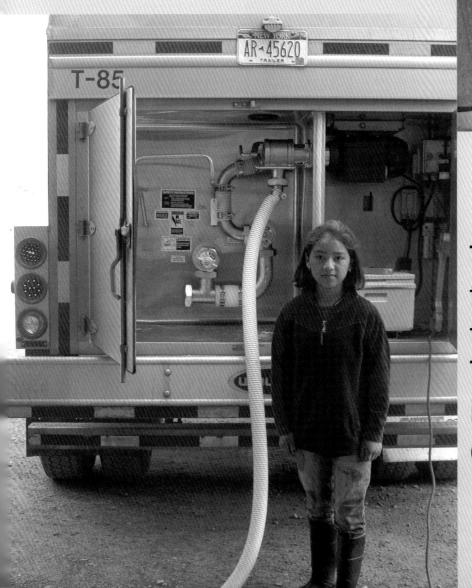

The milk truck comes to pump the milk from our bulk tank and take it to the processing plant. That's where our milk gets put in cartons or made into butter or ice cream!

I can help mix the milk
for the calves.

Some farms feed their calves milk from the milking machine. Other farms find that their calves do better on special formula designed for calves that we mix in buckets.

I can help feed the calves.

Calves are kept in pens. They are kept in different pens according to their age. The younger calves get their milk in buckets.

I can give the bottle to the calf.

This is my favorite job!

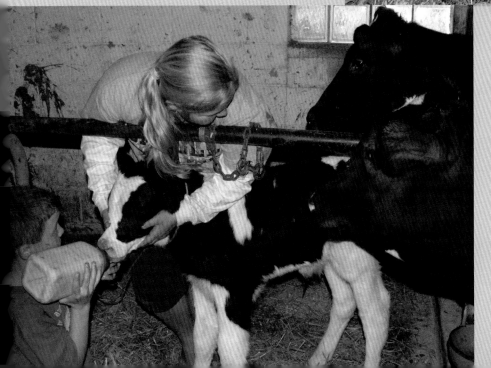

The newborn calves are kept near their mothers and are given their mother's milk which contains colostrum. This helps the calf resist diseases. The colostrum is not like milk, it's really sticky!

I can help feed the cows.

Cows eat 50 to 70 pounds of grain, corn and hay each day.

They also have automatic waterers, which are like drinking fountains. Each time the cow drinks, she pushes a lever which refills the fountain.

Our cows go outside during the summer to eat grass in the pasture.

I can bring hay to the cows.

We feed our cows both square bales and round bales.

A tractor has to bring the round bales.
They're too big to carry!

I can help get sawdust
for bedding.

The sawdust is kept in the barn loft. Every day, we shovel bedding down to put under the cows so that they are clean and comfortable when they lay down.

I can help bring the cows
in from the pasture.

Our cows go out in the pasture in the spring and summer when there is grass to eat.

When I bring them in, I don't yell or hit them. I walk very quietly and move them gently. We want our cows to be calm and to trust us.

I can help care for our cows
in many ways!

Our cows all have names. Some have been here since before I was born! Big farms can't always keep their older cows, but we are proud of our matron cows.

We keep our cows comfortable by brushing them
and petting them.

I can play in the hay loft.

Our loft is over the part of the barn where we keep our cows. I like to climb on the hay and play basketball!

We play up here a lot!

I can help feed our rabbits
and chickens.

Many dairy farms also have other animals, such as chickens, pigs, horses, or rabbits. A dairy farmer must be there on the farm every day to take care of the cows, so it is easy to keep other animals as well.

I can help plant our garden.

The tractor plows the fields where we grow all the food for the cows. But we have a garden where we grow food for us, too! I help plant the seeds and hoe the weeds.

I like to eat vegetables that we grow in our own garden!

I can get my calf ready to show.

Showing a cow or calf at a county or state fair is something children look forward to. Every year, we choose a calf that we work with to get her ready to show.

We also show our cows. It takes a lot of preparation to show a beautiful cow! We're proud of our cows!

I really like helping on the farm!

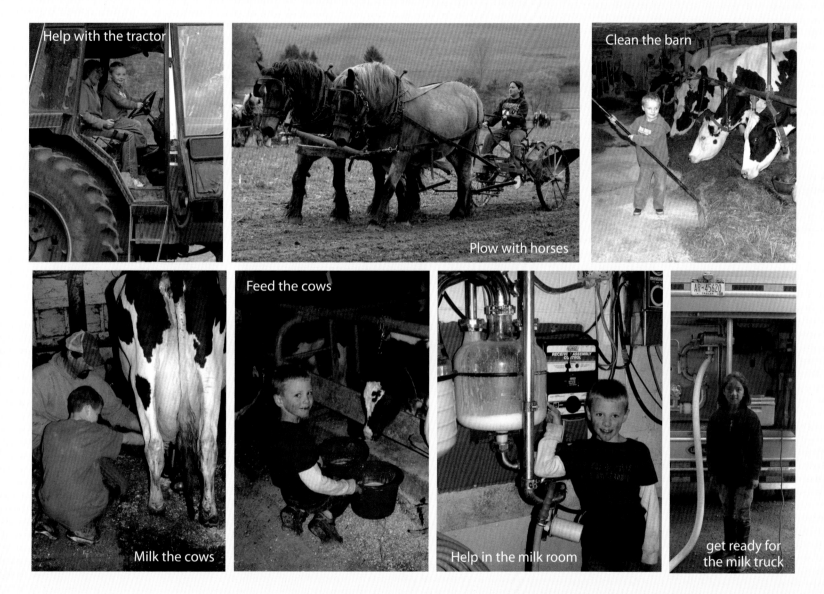

Help with the tractor

Plow with horses

Clean the barn

Milk the cows

Feed the cows

Help in the milk room

get ready for the milk truck

1. 15 jobs, 2. With a team of horses, 3. The machine is safer, faster and keeps the milk cleaner, 4. 7 1/2 gallons a day 5. 50 to 70 pounds of corn, grain, hay and grass a day, 6. Brushing and petting, putting down bedding, using iodine to prevent infections, feeding, 7. Rabbits, chickens, pigs, horses as well as cats and dogs, 8. Grow crops for food, raise cows for milk, take care of the land, 9. All of them!

Mix milk for the calves

Feed the calves

Give the young calves a bottle

Feed the other animals

Bring hay to the cows

Get sawdust for bedding

Bring cows in

plant and harvest a garden

How Much Do You Remember?

Below are some fun questions from the book. See how many you get right.
To check out the answers, see page 43.

1. How many jobs can you remember that children do on the farm?

2. How were fields plowed and harvested before we had tractors?

3. Why is it safer to use milking machines than to milk by hand?

4. About how many gallons of milk does a cow give each day?

5. About how much is a cow fed each day?

6. What are some things farmers do to keep their cows healthy and comfortable?

7. What other animals may live on a farm?

8. How do farmers help all of us?

9. What job would YOU like to do on the farm?

10. Circle all the foods that have milk in them!

Shells and cheese   Chocolate milk   Cheeseburger
        Caesar salad   Pudding   Cheese omelet
Yogurt   Fruit smoothie made with milk or yogurt   Taco with cheese
        Burrito   Cream soups   Ice cream
Cheese   Milk shake   Whipped cream
        Mozzarella sticks   Cereal with milk   Sour cream
                Shortbread   Butter cream frosting

Fun Facts:

The American Dietetic Association recommends three servings (8oz) of milk a day.

Milk and milk products contain many nutrients you need to help you grow strong and healthy, including:

Calcium: For strong bones and teeth,
Vitamin D: For a healthy heart and immune system,
Riboflavin: For converting food into energy,
Protein: To build muscle, Phosphorus, Vitamins B-12 and A, Potassium and Niacin: All needed to keep the body healthy and strong!

Order Page

Quantity		Price Total
_____ I Can Help on the Farm,	$14.95	_____
_____ Dreams on the Oregon Trail,	$14.95	_____
Shipping & Handling	($3.00 per book)	_____
Total		_____

Shipping Information:

Name: _____

Ship To Address: _____

City: _____

State/Zip: _____

Autograph Information:

_____ Autograph my Books, at No Additional Cost

Autograph to: _____

Mail your order to:

I Can Help on the Farm
2910 Avery Road,
North Brookfield, NY 13418

Please make checks payable to Barbara Linsley